"As I look back upon my life, there was nothing that happened to me that even approaches the experience I had with the Tuskegee Airmen."

—Benjamin O. Davis Jr. (1912–2002)

THE TUSKEGEE AIRMEN: AFRICAN-AMERICAN PILOTS OF WORLD WAR II

BY SARAH E. DE CAPUA

Content Reviewer: William F. Holton, National Historian, Tuskegee Airmen Incorporated

Published in the United States of America by The Child's World®
PO Box 326
Chanhassen, MN 55317-0326
800-599-READ
www.childsworld.com

The Child's World®: Mary Berendes, Publishing Director
Editorial Directions, Inc.: E. Russell Primm and Emily Dolbear, Editors; Katie Marsico and
Elizabeth K. Martin, Editorial Assistants; Dawn Friedman, Photo Researcher; Linda S. Koutris,
Photo Selector; Kerry Reid, Fact Researcher; Susan Hindman, Copy Editor; Lucia Raatma,
Proofreader; Tim Griffin/IndexServ, Indexer; Vicki Fischman, Page Production

Cover photograph: Tuskegee Airmen in Italy ca. 1940s/ ©Bettmann/Corbis

Interior photographs ©: Air Force Historical Research Agency—Maxwell Air Force Base, AL: 11, 12, 14, 24;
AP/Wide World Photos: 17, 20; Bettmann/Corbis: 2, 21, 26, 27, 28, 32, 33, 34; Corbis: 8, 19, 35; Oscar
White/Corbis: 9; Hulton-Deutsch Collection/Corbis: 18, 30 31; Ron Sachs/Corbis Sygma: 36; Hulton
Archive/Getty Images: 6, 13, 15, 23, 29; Library of Congress: 10, 22; Library of Congress, Prints &
Photographs Division, Toni Frissell Collection (LC-F9-4503-325-2): 16.

Library of Congress Cataloging-in-Publication Data
De Capua, Sarah.
The Tuskegee airmen : African-American pilots of World War II / by Sarah E. DeCapua.
p. cm. — (Journey to freedom)
Includes index.
ISBN 1-56766-550-0 (lib. bdg. : alk. paper)
1. World War, 1939–1945—Participation, African American—Juvenile literature. 2. Tuskegee Army Air Field
(Ala.)—Juvenile literature. 3. Moton Field—Juvenile literature. 4. African American soldiers—History—
Juvenile literature. 5. African American air pilots—Juvenile literature. 6. World War, 1939–1945—Aerial
operations, American—Juvenile literature. I. Title. II. Series.
D810.N4D4 2003
940.54'4973—dc21

2003004296

Contents

Preparing for War

By the late 1930s, events in Europe made it clear that a second world war was coming. Germany's Adolf Hitler and his Nazis had taken over Austria, Czechoslovakia, and Poland. The United States, England, France, Germany, and Japan were all preparing for war. They were building up their armed forces for combat on land, on the sea—and in the air.

As the United States prepared for war, any man in the country who wanted to be a military pilot had to apply to either the U.S. Army or the U.S. Navy. (The U.S. Air Force didn't become a separate branch of the military until 1947.) Within the army was a section called the Army Air Corps. The air corps, however, was closed to black pilots.

GERMAN TROOPS DURING THE INVASION OF PRAGUE, CZECHOSLOVAKIA. IN THE LATE 1930S, MANY NATIONS WERE PREPARING FOR WORLD WAR II.

Congress passed the **Civilian** Pilot Training Act in 1939. This law established the Civilian Pilot Training Program (CPTP) at colleges and universities across the country. The CPTP would provide pilot training to 20,000 college students each year. The goal was to build up a force of civilian pilots who could serve as military pilots during a war. The Civil Aeronautics Administration would supervise the program. Training was not available at all-black colleges.

THESE YOUNG MEN—AND THOUSANDS OF OTHER COLLEGE STUDENTS—TOOK PART IN THE CIVILIAN PILOT TRAINING PROGRAM.

In 1939, more than 200 black pilots were already licensed in the United States. Yet, there were very few opportunities for them to contribute to the war effort. As war in Europe grew closer, African-Americans wanted more than ever to join the armed forces as pilots.

The law in time was changed to allow African-Americans to train as pilots at certain black universities and colleges. Later, they were permitted to train specifically in preparation for duty in the U.S. Army Air Corps. Congress authorized funding for training at several black institutions, including the Tuskegee Institute. Founded by famous educator Booker T. Washington in 1881, the Tuskegee Institute (now called Tuskegee University) was a college in rural Alabama for black men and women.

BOOKER T. WASHINGTON FOUNDED THE TUSKEGEE INSTITUTE IN 1881. THIS COLLEGE WAS ONE OF THE FIRST TO OFFER TRAINING FOR BLACK PILOTS.

In early 1941, the air corps announced that blacks could become military pilots, and the War Department created the all-black 99th Fighter **Squadron.** Known for their skill and bravery, fighter pilots had the most respected job in the military. Their duties included attacking enemy fighter planes that threatened American **bombers** and destroying enemy targets on land and sea. Training would take place near the Tuskegee Institute at the Tuskegee Army Air Field. It had not yet been built but was completed soon after the air corps announcement.

STUDENTS IN A CLASS AT THE TUSKEGEE INSTITUTE. THE TUSKEGEE AIR FIELD WAS BUILT NEAR THIS COLLEGE SO PILOTS COULD BE TRAINED FOR THE MILITARY.

Setting Up the Experiment

The Army Air Corps chose to set up its black military pilot training base near the Tuskegee Institute because of the school's excellent record in the Civilian Pilot Training Program. Every member of the CPTP training class had received good grades, passed the flight test, and earned his pilot's license.

After the Tuskegee Army Air Field was built, applications for the official air corps training program were received and acceptances mailed. Tuskegee's chief flight instructor was Charles Alfred Anderson. In July 1933, Anderson and Albert E. Forsythe had become the first black pilots to complete round-trip flights between Atlantic City, New Jersey, and Los Angeles, California. That same year, they flew to Canada.

CHARLES ALFRED ANDERSON (SECOND FROM RIGHT) WAS THE CHIEF FLIGHT INSTRUCTOR AT TUSKEGEE.

Tuskegee Army Air Field provided the same facilities and training to the Tuskegee **cadets** as it did to whites. The base included offices and a headquarters. There were runways, barracks (where the cadets lived), and mess halls (where the cadets and officers ate meals). A hospital, hangars (buildings where planes are stored), theater, and exchange (a type of store) were also built.

THE TUSKEGEE ARMY AIR FIELD SEEN FROM ABOVE. IT WAS AN ELABORATE GROUP OF RUNWAYS, BARRACKS, HANGARS, AND OFFICES.

The institute and the airfield were located only 6 miles (10 kilometers) from the town of Tuskegee, Alabama. **Segregation** and **discrimination** were still a way of life in the South at that time. The town's restaurants and one movie theater had separate entrances and seating areas for African-Americans. Water fountains and public rest rooms were segregated, too. Signs labeled "Whites Only" or "Colored" were common.

AN AFRICAN-AMERICAN MAN USING A SEPARATE ENTRANCE TO A MOVIE THEATER. SUCH UNFAIR RESTRICTIONS AGAINST BLACK AMERICANS WERE ALL TOO COMMON.

The townspeople didn't welcome the pilot training program or the cadets. As a result, the black trainees depended on one another for support, encouragement, and guidance. The base offered sports teams, art exhibits, and other forms of entertainment, so cadets and officers rarely left the grounds.

The Tuskegee Experiment—the air corps's name for the program that would determine if blacks had the ability, intelligence, and courage to be military pilots—was about to begin. U.S. military leaders expected the experiment to fail. The pilot trainees, however, were determined to see that it didn't.

THESE BARRACKS WERE HOME TO THE CADETS AT TUSKEGEE ARMY AIR FIELD. UNWELCOME BY THE PEOPLE OF TUSKEGEE, THE TRAINEES OFTEN STAYED ON THE GROUNDS.

Training and Flight

On July 19, 1941, the first class of black pilot trainees arrived at the Tuskegee Institute. Known as Class 42C, it consisted of 12 cadets and one army officer. These cadets were all college graduates and included a policeman and a factory worker. The army officer was Captain Benjamin O. Davis Jr., a graduate of the U.S. Military Academy at West Point. He was the son of Benjamin O. Davis Sr., who was the first black general in the U.S. Army.

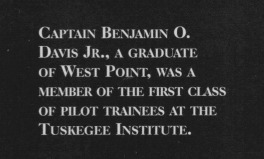

CAPTAIN BENJAMIN O. DAVIS JR., A GRADUATE OF WEST POINT, WAS A MEMBER OF THE FIRST CLASS OF PILOT TRAINEES AT THE TUSKEGEE INSTITUTE.

Training for Class 42C began as soon as the cadets arrived. Under the direction of Captain Noel Parrish, the training consisted of three parts: primary, basic, and advanced. Primary and basic training included ground school. In ground school, the cadets studied the science and engineering needed to be pilots. They learned what makes a plane fly, how weather affects a plane's flight, and how to read flight maps and to **navigate.**

Advanced training consisted of military flying. The cadets learned how to change a plane's direction, speed, and elevation. Cadets flew with an instructor in the backseat. They practiced takeoffs, landings, and maneuvers.

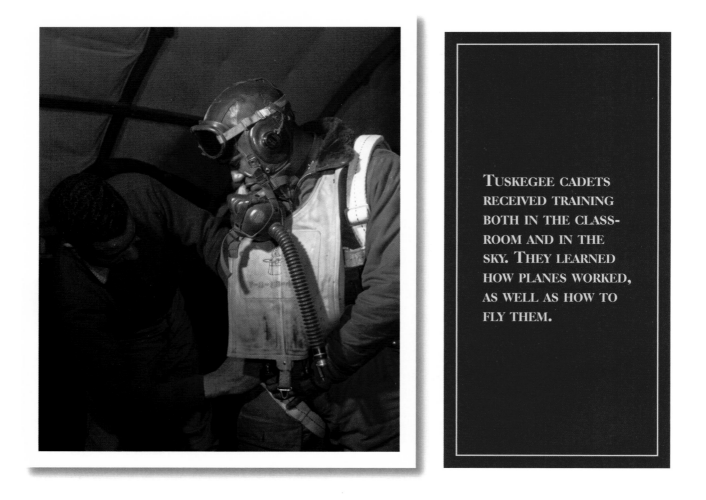

TUSKEGEE CADETS RECEIVED TRAINING BOTH IN THE CLASS-ROOM AND IN THE SKY. THEY LEARNED HOW PLANES WORKED, AS WELL AS HOW TO FLY THEM.

After eight hours of flight instruction, each cadet performed a solo flight. He took off, flew, and landed the plane by himself. On September 2, 1941, Benjamin O. Davis Jr. officially became the first black officer to solo in an Army Air Corps aircraft.

Fighter pilot training, which began after cadets had learned how to fly, consisted of learning to strafe. Strafing means flying low and firing the plane's machine guns at ground targets. Pilots also learned to shoot at targets in the sky by firing at banners towed by other aircraft.

AFTER LEARNING HOW TO FLY PLANES LIKE THIS ONE, FIGHTER PILOTS THEN MASTERED ATTACKING GROUND TARGETS.

ive men from Class 42C completed the training. On March 7, 1942, the five marched onto the Tuskegee Army Air Field runway in a ceremony to mark the occasion. Lemuel Custis, Charles DeBow, George Roberts, and Mac Ross were commissioned second lieutenants in the Army Air Force. (The Army Air Corps had become the Army Air Force in June 1941.) Davis, an army captain, became an air force captain.

THE FIVE MEMBERS OF THE FIRST GRADUATING CLASS AT THE TUSKEGEE INSTITUTE WITH ONE OF THEIR INSTRUCTORS (FROM LEFT TO RIGHT): GEORGE ROBERTS, BENJAMIN O. DAVIS JR., CHARLES DEBOW, INSTRUCTOR R. M. LONG, MAC ROSS, AND LEMUEL CUSTIS.

The officers received their silver pilot wings, indicating that they were officially pilots—the first of their race in the Army Air Force. They were the first Tuskegee Airmen.

Other cadets followed them through the training. As each class graduated, the pilots were assigned to the 99th Fighter Squadron. The 100th Fighter Squadron was established in May 1942, in anticipation of the growing number of fliers who would graduate from the program. Lieutenant Ross was appointed commander of the 100th. Davis, who had been promoted to lieutenant colonel, was made the commanding officer of the 99th.

A GROUP OF CADETS IN NAVIGATION CLASS, SEPTEMBER 1942. MANY YOUNG MEN FOLLOWED THE EXAMPLE OF THOSE FIRST FIVE GRADUATES AND WENT ON TO BECOME PILOTS.

On December 7, 1941, Japanese bombers attacked a military base in Pearl Harbor, Hawaii. Soon after, the United States entered World War II. By the spring of 1942, the pilots of the 99th were proud of how far they had come. They were ready for combat. They waited for the orders that would send them to war against Hitler's Nazis. During that time, they continued to practice and perfect their flying skills.

SOME OF THE WRECKAGE AT PEARL HARBOR, HAWAII. JAPANESE FIGHTERS ATTACKED THIS U.S. MILITARY BASE ON DECEMBER 7, 1941.

Near the end of 1942, Noel Parrish (by then promoted to colonel) grew tired of waiting for his pilots to receive orders. He flew to Washington, D.C., and met with Undersecretary of War for Air Robert Leavitt at the War Department. There, Parrish strongly urged sending his men overseas to contribute to the war effort. He knew they were prepared for the challenge.

THE WAR DEPARTMENT BUILDING IN WASHINGTON, D.C. IT WAS THERE THAT COLONEL PARRISH ARGUED IN FAVOR OF SENDING THE TUSKEGEE AIRMEN INTO COMBAT.

Finally, on April 1, 1943, the 400 members of the 99th Fighter Squadron received their orders. The following day, the 99th left Tuskegee bound for New York, where they would board a troop ship that would take them across the Atlantic Ocean to the war in North Africa and Europe. Colonel Parrish, who had always believed in the men of the 99th, reminded them that their future depended "on how determined you are not to give satisfaction to those who would like to see you fail."

AFRICAN-AMERICAN TROOPS ONBOARD A MILITARY SHIP. THE TUSKEGEE AIRMEN WERE EAGER TO SHOW HOW PREPARED THEY WERE FOR BATTLE.

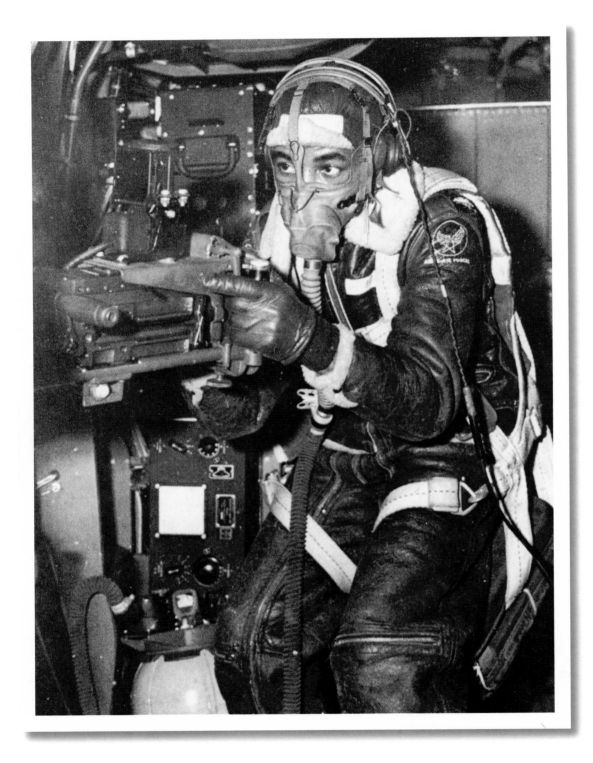

Proving Themselves

During their service, the Tuskegee Airmen proved that the experiment was a huge success. The 99th arrived at Casablanca, Morocco, in North Africa, on April 24, 1943. They trained in Morocco for a month in brand-new P-40 Warhawk planes before they were moved to a combat base in Tunisia. Their duties included guiding bombers and ship **convoys,** protecting them from enemy fighter planes, and strafing enemy targets, such as bridges and truck convoys.

On June 2, 1943, the pilots of the 99th experienced their first combat while leading bombers from the Italian island of Pantelleria. It was on that day that the pilots spotted a group of German fighters, which engaged them in combat. All the planes of the 99th returned safely to base. One month later, led by Lieutenant Charles Hall, the squadron scored its first aerial victory when Hall shot down a German fighter.

A GUNNER KEEPING AN EYE ON HIS TARGET. FIGHTER PILOTS WERE TRAINED TO FLY AS WELL AS TO ATTACK.

The 99th moved from North Africa to the southern coast of Sicily, an Italian island that is located in the Mediterranean Sea and almost touches the toe of Italy's boot. Throughout July and August, the squadron helped American troops advance through Sicily.

THE TUSKEGEE PILOTS IN ITALY. THE EFFORTS OF THESE MEN ENABLED U.S. TROOPS TO GAIN GROUND IN SICILY.

In spite of the fine work and fighting ability shown by the black pilots, army leaders continued to oppose the squadron's involvement in the war. Colonel William Momyer was the commander of the white 33rd Fighter Group to which the 99th was joined. Momyer told U.S. Army leaders that the 99th was not as good as the other fighter squadrons in the group. When word got out, *Time* magazine's September 20, 1943, issue featured an article that suggested top air commanders were about to remove the 99th from combat duty.

Rumors that the 99th would be grounded disturbed Colonel Benjamin O. Davis Jr. He had returned to the United States to command the all-black 332nd Fighter Group, which was training in Michigan. He spoke before a War Department committee, defending the abilities and combat record of the pilots.

COLONEL BENJAMIN O. DAVIS JR. APPEARED WITH HIS FATHER BEFORE A WAR DEPARTMENT COMMITTEE AND DEFENDED THE 99TH FIGHTER SQUADRON.

In reaction to this controversy, Army Chief of Staff General George Marshall ordered a review to assess the pilots' performances. The review showed the 99th was equal to, if not better than, white fighter squadrons with similar experience in the war zone.

GENERAL GEORGE MARSHALL, WHO SERVED AS ARMY CHIEF OF STAFF, ORDERED A REVIEW OF THE 99TH FIGHTER SQUADRON. THE RESULTS OF THE REVIEW PROVED THAT THE PILOTS' PERFORMANCE MATCHED OR EXCEEDED THAT OF WHITE SQUADRONS.

The 99th was later attached to the 79th Fighter Group under Colonel Earl E. Bates, who integrated, or combined, the groups. The 79th pilots were required to fly with those of the 99th, and the 99th pilots were ordered to fly with those of the 79th. The 99th pilots began to feel accepted. They knew that they were finally contributing to the war effort.

BEFORE LONG, THE PILOTS OF THE 99TH WERE INTEGRATED WITH THE PILOTS OF THE 79TH FIGHTER SQUADRON. ONCE IN THE SKY, THESE MEN LEARNED TO ACCEPT ONE ANOTHER.

U.S. TROOPS DURING THE INVASION OF ANZIO, ITALY. THE 99TH HELPED
FIGHT THE GERMANS AND MADE THE INVASION A SUCCESS.

Hard-Won Recognition

On January 22, 1944, the 99th Fighter Squadron began covering the **Allied** invasion of Anzio, Italy. On January 27, the squadron foughta group of German fighters. Five enemy planes were shot down. Later that day, three more enemy planes were destroyed. Only one 99th pilot was killed.

These events proved to be a turning point for the 99th. Three days later, more German planes were shot down. The 99th began receiving more positive recognition for its achievements. The pilots had shown they could succeed in air combat.

Through February 1944, the 99th victory totals continued to mount. News of their victories was carried in newspapers, on the radio, and in **newsreels** throughout the United States. Army Air Force leaders who had expected them to fail accepted that they had earned a place of honor in the war.

CAMERA OPERATORS THROUGHOUT EUROPE CAPTURED THE ACTION FOR NEWSREELS THAT WERE SHOWN ALL OVER THE UNITED STATES.

In February 1944, Colonel Davis returned to the **front** with the all-black 332nd Fighter Group. In June, Davis's men were assigned to protect the crews of bombers on missions to enemy territory, where they were to destroy German bunkers and air fields on the ground. Davis's men flew P-51s, the best fighter planes in the Army Air Force. They painted the tails of the planes red, earning them the nickname Red Tails.

The air force bombers welcomed the Red Tails. Bomber crews admired the skill of the Red Tail pilots. In fact, no bomber accompanied by the Red Tails was lost to enemy fighters during the time the 99th Fighter Squadron operated with them.

IN THE MILITARY, DIFFERENT KINDS OF PLANES HAVE DIFFERENT PURPOSES. FIGHTER PLANES OFFER PROTECTION TO AIR FORCE BOMBERS.

No escort group's record equaled that of the Red Tails. While other pilots flew only 50 missions before returning to the United States, Tuskegee Airmen flew close to 100 missions because of the lack of replacement pilots. The challenge increased their chances of injury and death.

The Red Tails flew their final mission on April 30, 1945. The war ended in Europe eight days later. Training at the Tuskegee Army Air Field ended in 1946.

WHEN WORLD WAR II ENDED, THOUSANDS OF AMERICANS WELCOMED THE TROOPS HOME.

Of the 996 pilots who graduated from Tuskegee, 450 were sent overseas. Of that number, 32 were shot down and became prisoners of war, and 66 were killed in action. The pilots of the 332nd were rewarded for their distinguished combat record. They received 95 Distinguished Flying Crosses, 14 Bronze Stars, and eight Purple Hearts, among other medals and honors.

The Distinguished Flying Cross is a medal awarded to those showing heroism or extraordinary achievement while flying an aircraft. The Bronze Star is a medal awarded for heroic service or achievement that does not involve flying an aircraft. The Purple Heart is a medal awarded to members of the armed forces who are wounded or killed in action.

THE DISTINGUISHED FLYING CROSS. THIS HONOR IS AWARDED TO THOSE WHO SHOW HEROISM WHILE FLYING AN AIRCRAFT. MEMBERS OF THE 332ND RECEIVED 95 DISTINGUISHED FLYING CROSSES.

Life Back Home

After World War II ended, the Tuskegee Airmen returned to a segregated United States. Even with their outstanding war records, the African-American pilots were treated as second-class citizens. A life of segregation back home was difficult for them to accept. They became determined to win a victory over segregation and discrimination just as they had helped to win victory over Adolf Hitler.

The Tuskegee Airmen's contribution to the civil rights movement was made clear in 1948. That year, President Harry S. Truman issued Executive Order 9981, which led to the integration of the American military. The order required equal treatment of soldiers, regardless of race. Executive Order 9981 was the foundation for future civil rights legislation, including the desegregation of public schools in 1954, the Civil Rights Act of 1964, and the Voting Rights Act of 1965.

MEMBERS OF AN INTEGRATED AMERICAN UNIT DURING THEIR SERVICE IN THE KOREAN WAR (1950–1953)

Today, it's hard to believe that African-Americans had to prove through an experiment that they had the same abilities as whites. Countless numbers of blacks have made outstanding contributions to military service. Perhaps the most notable example is General Colin Powell, who served as chairman of the **Joint Chiefs of Staff** before becoming the secretary of state under President George W. Bush in 2001. However, the lesser-known veterans of war in Korea, Vietnam, and the Persian Gulf, as well as astronauts and the cadets training at the U.S. military's service academies, carry on the legacy of the Tuskegee Airmen.

GENERAL COLIN POWELL IS ONE OF THE MOST RESPECTED LEADERS IN THE UNITED STATES. HE SERVED AS CHAIRMAN OF THE JOINT CHIEFS OF STAFF AND BECAME SECRETARY OF STATE IN 2001.

Timeline

1881 Booker T. Washington founds the Tuskegee Institute near Tuskegee, Alabama.

1933 Charles Alfred Anderson and Albert E. Forsythe make several long-distance and transcontinental flights. They become the first black pilots to complete round-trip flights between Atlantic City, New Jersey, and Los Angeles, California.

1939 Congress passes the Civilian Pilot Training Act. The National Airmen's Association of America is founded in Chicago. More than 200 black pilots are licensed in the United States.

1941 The Army Air Corps permits the training of black pilots and establishes the 99th Fighter Squadron. Class 42C arrives at the Tuskegee Institute on July 19. Captain Benjamin O. Davis Jr. officially becomes the first black officer to solo in an Army Air Corps aircraft on September 2. On December 7, the Japanese attack Pearl Harbor, Hawaii, drawing the United States into World War II.

1942 On March 7, Lemuel Custis, Charles DeBow, George Roberts, Mac Ross, and Benjamin O. Davis Jr. of Class 42C receive their silver pilot wings and become the first official African-American pilots in the Army Air Force. In May, the 100th Fighter Squadron is established.

1943 The 99th Fighter Squadron joins the war effort in Europe. On June 2, pilots of the 99th experience their first combat while leading bombers from the Italian island of Pantelleria.

1944 Members of the 332nd Fighter Group, called the Red Tails, distinguish themselves on bomber escort missions.

1945 The Red Tails fly their final mission on April 30. World War II ends.

1946 Training at Tuskegee ends.

1947 The U.S. Air Force becomes a separate branch of the military.

1948 President Harry S. Truman issues Executive Order 9981, which leads to the integration of the U.S. military.

1959 Tuskegee Airman Benjamin O. Davis Jr. becomes the first black general in the U.S. Air Force.

Glossary

Allied (AL-lide)
People or groups that join together for a common cause are allied. In World War II, the Allied forces were made up of troops from the United States, Great Britain, France, and Russia. They fought against the Axis forces, made up of troops from Germany, Italy, and Japan.

bombers (BOM-urs)
Bombers are airplanes that drop bombs on targets. The planes of the 99th surrounded American bombers to protect them from attack by German fighter planes.

cadets (kuh-DETS)
Young people who are training to become members of the armed forces are called cadets. The first 12 black pilot cadets arrived at the Tuskegee Institute on July 19, 1941.

civilian (si-VIL-yuhn)
A civilian is someone who is not a member of the armed forces. The Civilian Pilot Training Program built up a force of civilian pilots who could serve as military pilots during a war.

convoys (KON-voys)
Convoys are groups of ships, military vehicles, or trucks that are traveling together. The 99th Fighter Squadron flew above ship convoys to protect them from attack by German fighter planes.

discrimination (diss-krim-i-NAY-shun)
Discrimination is prejudice or unfair behavior toward others based on race, age, gender, or other factors. The black pilot cadets faced discrimination in the Alabama town of Tuskegee.

front (fruhnt)
The front is the place where armies are fighting. Colonel Davis commanded the 332nd Fighter Group at the Italian front.

Joint Chiefs of Staff (JOYNT CHEEFS of STAF)
The Joint Chiefs of Staff is a group made up of the heads of the army, air force, navy, and marines, which advises the president. As chairman of the Joint Chiefs of Staff, General Colin Powell was the leader of this group.

navigate (NAV-uh-gate)
To navigate means to steer or control the course of a ship, an aircraft, or other vehicle using maps, compasses, the stars, or other means, for guidance. The Tuskegee cadets learned to navigate their planes in order to be effective pilots.

newsreels (NOOZ-reelz)
Newsreels are short movies dealing with current events. Before people had televisions in their homes, they got their news by watching newsreels in movie theaters.

segregation (seg-ruh-GAY-shun)
Segregation is the act or practice of keeping people or groups apart. Segregation was common in the South during the time of the Tuskegee Airmen's training.

squadron (SKWAHD-ruhn)
A squadron is a group of ships, cavalry troops, or other military units. The 99th Fighter Squadron consisted of black pilots and their aircraft.

Index

Further Information

Books

Adams, Simon. *World War II.* New York: Dorling Kindersley Publishing, 2000.

George, Linda, and Charles George. *The Tuskegee Airmen.* Danbury, Conn.: Children's Press, 2001.

Jones, Stanley P. *African-American Aviators.* Mankato, Minn.: Capstone Press, 1998.

Jones, Steven L. *The Red Tails: World War II's Tuskegee Airmen.* Logan, Iowa: Perfection Learning, 2002.

Web Sites

Visit our homepage for lots of links about the Tuskegee Airmen:

http://www.childsworld.com/links.html

Note to Parents, Teachers, and Librarians:
We routinely verify our Web links to make sure they're safe, active sites—so encourage your readers to check them out!

About the Author

Sarah De Capua has always been impressed by the contributions of the Tuskegee Airmen who helped to win World War II. While researching this book, she enjoyed visiting various sites and memorials dedicated to preserving the legacy of the airmen's achievements. Born and raised in Connecticut, De Capua currently resides in Colorado.

J
940.54
D

De Capua, Sarah.

The Tuskegee airmen.

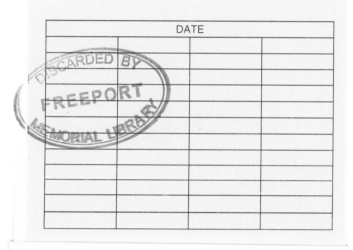
BAKER & TAYLOR